I0429797

THE BOOK OF IDEAS /
THE GENIUS GUIDE TO GENIUS

AN INDEXICAL GUIDE DE-
SIGNED TO ASSIST IN THE
SEARCH FOR NEW CATE-
GORIES OF INNOVATIVE
REASONING

By Nathan Coppedge

Nathan Coppedge

All content
© 2014, 2015 Nathan Coppedge

TABLE OF CONTENTS

≈INTRODUCTION≈

The approach used in this guide is a more fluid version of advanced techniques I used to invent the paroxysm or double-paradox, categorical deduction method, and aperrature or mobile building concept, and other similar simple yet brilliant principles.

Keep in mind that the way this guide is designed, big ideas can be very small footnotes buried in individual one-line descriptions.

This guide is designed for discovering new sources of insight when the proverbial wells run dry. Whether someone needs prophetic advice, a new innovative idea, or some help with brainstorming, this book is not a planner, but rather a do-it-yourself sourcebook. Although the entries are repetitive, there is genius at work. The twenty categories cover themes which range from *existentia*, to conditionalities, to definitionalities. The themes are designed to overlap only by creating new categories, thus serving as a kind of 'genius guide to genius.'

Simple and complex definitions of category are included, with the aim of being totally comprehensive of the past, present, and future body of ideas, across disciplines, and in every nation on the globe.

Advice on the Original Content: Don't read linearly. Instead, spot-read with a critical mind. When you run out of steam, look up the closest category to what you are thinking by choosing one word twice from the word list in the Table of Contents. The words are designed to combine exponentially. Refer to the entry listing the first word's number followed by the second word's number. When you have found the result, which should be a one-line description within the body of the book, begin brainstorming about what this particular expression might mean for your project. If you don't feel inspired the first time, try a few more times for practice.

There is also a list of ideas already constructed for you, in case you want to cut to the quick. Those are listed on pages 29 - 31.

Also feel free to glance at the additional notes listed in the index, and located at the end of the book. These sections are for extra inspiration.

THE BOOK
OF IDEAS

Nathan Coppedge

I. WORK

II. IMPOSSIBILITY

III. MECHANATION

IV. TELEOLOGY

4.1 Working on Causation

4.2 An Impossible Causation

4.3 The Machine of Causation

4.4 Causing / Involving Causation

4.5 Perfect Causation

4.6 Real Causation

4.7 Powerful Causation

4.8 Theoretical Causation

4.9 Fortunate Causation

4.10 Artistic Causation

4.11 Destroying Causation

4.12 Humble Causation

4.13 Fallacious Causation

4.14 Decayed Causation

4.15 Fantastic Causation

4.16 Complex Causation

4.17 Surprising Causation

4.18 Natural Causation

4.19 Omnipotent Causation

4.20 Leisurely Causation

V. PERFECTION

5.1 Working on Perfection
5.2 An Impossible Perfection
5.3 The Machine of Perfection
5.4 Causing / Involving Perfection
5.5 Perfect Perfection
5.6 Real Perfection
5.7 Powerful Perfection
5.8 Theoretical Perfection
5.9 Fortunate Perfection
5.10 Artistic Perfection
5.11 Destroying Perfection
5.12 Humble Perfection
5.13 Fallacious Perfection
5.14 Decayed Perfection
5.15 Fantastic Perfection
5.16 Complex Perfection
5.17 Surprising Perfection
5.18 Natural Perfection
5.19 Omnipotent Perfection
5.20 Leisurely Perfection

VI. REALISM

VII. POWER

VIII. THEORY

8.1 Working on Theory
8.2 An Impossible Theory
8.3 The Machine of Theories
8.4 Causing / Involving Theory
8.5 The Perfect Theory
8.6 The Real Theory
8.7 The Powerful Theory
8.8 Theoretical Theory
8.9 Fortunate Theory
8.10 Artistic Theory
8.11 Destroying Theory
8.12 Humble Theory
8.13 Fallacious Theory
8.14 Decayed Theory
8.15 Fantastic Theory
8.16 Complex Theory
8.17 Surprising Theory
8.18 Natural Theory
8.19 Omnipotent Theory
8.20 Leisurely Theory

IX. FORTUNE

9.1 Working on Fortune

9.2 An Impossible Fortune

9.3 The Machine of Fortune

9.4 Causing / Involving Fortune

9.5 The Perfect Fortune

9.6 The Real Fortune

9.7 The Powerful Fortune

9.8 Theoretical Fortune

9.9 Fortunate Fortune

9.10 Artistic Fortune

9.11 Destroying Fortune

9.12 Humble Fortune

9.13 Fallacious Fortune

9.14 Decayed Fortune

9.15 Fantastic Fortune

9.16 Complex Fortune

9.17 Surprising Fortune

9.18 Natural Fortune

9.19 Omnipotent Fortune

9.20 Leisurely Fortune

X. ART

XI. DESTRUCTION

11.1 Working on Destruction
11.2 An Impossible Destruction
11.3 The Machine of Destruction
11.4 Causing / Involving Destruction
11.5 The Perfect Destruction
11.6 The Real Destruction
11.7 The Powerful Destruction
11.8 Theoretical Destruction
11.9 Fortunate Destruction
11.10 Artistic Destruction
11.11 Destroying Destruction
11.12 Humble Destruction
11.13 Fallacious Destruction
11.14 Decayed Destruction
11.15 Fantastic Destruction
11.16 Complex Destruction
11.17 Surprising Destruction
11.18 Natural Destruction
11.19 Omnipotent Destruction
11.20 Leisurely Destruction

XII. HUMILITY

XIII. FOLLY

XIV. DECAY

14.1 Working on Decay
14.2 An Impossible Decay
14.3 A Decaying Machine
14.4 Causing / Involving Decay
14.5 The Perfectly Decayed
14.6 The Really Decayed
14.7 The Powerfully Decayed
14.8 A Theoretical Decay
14.9 A Fortunate Decay
14.10 An Artistic Decay
14.11 The Destruction of Decay
14.12 Humble Decay
14.13 Fallacious Decay
14.14 Decayed Decay
14.15 Fantastic Decay
14.16 Complex Decay
14.17 Surprising Decay
14.18 Natural Decay
14.19 Omnipotent Decay
14.20 Leisurely Decay

XV. FANTASY

15.1 Working on a Fantasy
15.2 An Impossible Fantasy
15.3 A Fantastic Machine
15.4 Causing / Involving Fantasy
15.5 The Perfect Fantasy
15.6 A Real Fantasy
15.7 A Powerful Fantasy
15.8 A Theoretical Fantasy
15.9 A Fortunate Fantasy
15.10 An Artistic Fantasy
15.11 The Destruction of Fantasy
15.12 Humble Fantasy
15.13 Fallacious Fantasy
15.14 Decayed Fantasy
15.15 Fantastic Fantasy
15.16 Complex Fantasy
15.17 Surprising Fantasy
15.18 Natural Fantasy
15.19 Omnipotent Fantasy
15.20 Leisurely Fantasy

XVI. COMPLEXITY

XVII. SURPRISE

17.1 Working on a Surprise
17.2 An Impossible Surprise
17.3 A Mechanical Surprise
17.4 Causing / Involving Surprise
17.5 Perfect Surprise
17.6 Real Surprise
17.7 Powerful Surprise
17.8 Theoretical Surprise
17.9 Fortunate Surprise
17.10 Artistic Surprise
17.11 Destroyed by Surprise
17.12 Humble Surprise
17.13 Fallacious Surprise
17.14 Decayed Surprise
17.15 Fantastic Surprise
17.16 Complicated Surprise
17.17 Surprising Surprise
17.18 Natural Surprise
17.19 Omnipotent Surprise
17.20 Leisurely Surprise

XVIII. NATURE

18.1 Working on Nature
18.2 Impossible Nature
18.3 Nature the Machine
18.4 Causing / Involving Nature
18.5 Perfect Nature
18.6 Real Nature
18.7 Powerful Nature
18.8 Theoretical Nature
18.9 Fortunate Nature
18.10 Artistic Nature
18.11 Destructive Nature
18.12 Humble Nature
18.13 Natural Fallacies
18.14 Natural Decay
18.15 Natural Fantasies
18.16 Complex Nature
18.17 Surprising Nature
18.18 The Nature of Natures
18.19 Omnipotent Nature
18.20 Leisurely Nature

XIX. OMNIPOTENCE

XX. LEISURE

20.1 Working on Leisure
20.2 Impossible Leisure
20.3 Machines for Leisure
20.4 Causing / Involving Leisure
20.5 Perfect Leisure
20.6 Realistic Leisure
20.7 Powerful Leisure
20.8 Theoretical Leisure
20.9 Fortunate Leisure
20.10 Artistic Leisure
20.11 Leisure with Destruction
20.12 Humble Leisure
20.13 Fallacious Leisure
20.14 Decayed Leisure
20.15 Fantasies of Leisure
20.16 Complex Leisure
20.17 Surprising Leisure
20.18 Natural Leisure
20.19 Omnipotent Leisure
20.20 Leisure with Leisure

IDEAS

Shortlist: TECHNE

Critics of Nature
Pithy Resources
Patient Technology
Logic Systems
Orders of Nature
Functional Symbols
Positive Paradoxes
Happy People
Inspired Conventions
Green Techno-Sculpture
Technical Hobbies
Modular Law
Techno-Weaving
Pieces of Perfection
Functional Nothing
Words for the Wise
Picture Tables
Fortunate Rice
Weapons of Enjoyment
Enhanced Basics
Architecture Delusion
Frequency Locations
Processing Machines

SOCIETY & ECONOMICS

Virtual Economy
Free / Energy Economy
Modular Citizenship
Modular Government
Social Index Functions
Computer Infrastructure
Casual Jobs
Casual Industry
Virtual Business Jewelry
    'tiny screen, tells you
    what it means'
Service Packages
Knowledge Integration
Mass-Ecology Industry
Urban Zen

INTELLIGENCE

Double-Spiral Brain With
    Colexy
Irrational Rationality
Gray Epiphanies
Aesthetic Epicureanism

PHILOSOPHY
Paroxysm: Double-Paradox
Categorical Deduction Using
     Diagonal Opposites
     (A-B:C-D / A-D:C-B)
Exclusive Categories
Coherent Knowledge

ART & GRAPHICS

Hyper-Cubism (beyond
     Cubism)
Colloid / Polloid (hyper-figure,
     and coherent hyper-
     figure)
Visual Logic Parsing Using
     Category-Logic to
     Determine Symbols
Corruscation (Hyper-
     Dimensional Dynamic
     Style)

VIRTUAL REALITY
Intermediate Interface
Double-Interface
Click-Toggle Button
Categorical Metaphysics

PROJECTS
Create Infinitely Detailed Knowl-
edge
Make a Universe for Every Person
Create God
Turn the World into a Brain
Time Travel a Star
Make the Universe Invulnerable
Make Everything Related
Solve All Practical Problems
Create Science that Applies to
        Nonsense
Make All Life-Forms Think
Make Rationally Realistic Magic
Create Norms of Omniscience
Create Genuine Alternate Reality
Make Old-Fashioned Apps for
        Everyday Objects.
Augment the Human Soul
Create a Government that Works in
        Nature
Make Necessity Un-Necessary
Re-Invent Pain as Something More
        Pleasurable
Make All Jobs Idealistic
Edit the Meaning of Life
Discover Separate Realities

PROFOUND IDEAS

Apertures
World-Keys
Dimensional Doors
Folded Reality
Important Names
Extra Rooms
Added Contents
Technology Equipment
Special Considerations
Added License
Room for Improvement
Perfect Accommodations
Secret of Life
Trial-and-Error
Tested to Perfection
Rules for Fools (Frooles)
Corner the Market
Big Production
Perfect Setting
Magical Encounter
Spiritual Development
Infinite Patience
An Easing of His Heart
A Big Commitment
The Perfect Game
A Piece in the Puzzle

CONCEPTUAL TOOLS
Outside-of-Everything
System 2

ECONOMICS

The Dimensional Dollar: Money that markets the spender's services...

*Goods or services that the person provides (capital)
*Or, information or networks that the person grants access to (like sharing friends lists, or granting temporary access to a hive mind)
*Or, the person may provide a future market for capital management, therefore expanding the market offered by the business.
*In any case, there are gains, because either the dollar stays active and offers the person's services through the network (if it is not spent), or the person is offering some type of expanded service (by spending), or the person decides not to offer an expanded service, and therefore shows a weakness towards the market.

ADDITIONAL MATERIALS

Nathan Coppedge

Secret Combinations

Original-if-original can be productive!

I've thought of it before, so I-can-think-of-it-again-but-better is effective.

"Time is the miracle of problems."

Simple Shortcuts

Combining logical or organizational functions with practical or utility functions can result in easy access to a higher form of ideas.

For example, try combining 'Systemic', 'Process', 'Automatic', 'Exponential', 'Efficient', 'Corroborative', or 'Pithy'

With: 'Deduction', 'Product', 'Output', 'Function', 'Variable', 'Art-form', 'Conservation', 'Mechanism', or 'Pathway'

And the result is extreme!

An Extemporaneous Method

Example

"Let's start with the concept of 'interweaving'! Where can we go with it?"

"The proper term is 'mesh'. We ought to apply the concept of 'mesh'."

"Let's start with the basics. Perhaps this is unsolvable. But is matter 'meshed'?"

"What is the ideal type of mesh?"

"Does mesh involve an interpretive function?"

"Maybe a logical mesh has secondary functions, like 'labaryinthine,' and 'melding'..."

"It's obvious that mesh could serve a logical function, as the intermeshing of any two sets of concepts."

"Although mesh depends on which concepts those are, the right concepts could lead to the right mesh".

BIOLOGICAL IDEAS

Germ rock.

Heliophiles.

Extremophiles.

Symbiosis.

Co-adaptation.

Stings and other defenses.

War colors.

Problem-solving.

Mate selection by intelligence.
(Lamarckianism).

Leisure to think.

Extreme intelligence.

Computers and calculators.

Codified X, Y, Z and correlation.

HISTORICAL IDEAS

The Wheel
Heraclitus' Time
Pythagoras' Arithmetic
Parmenides' Permanence
Plato's Republic 400 BCE
Aristotle's Metaphysics
Protagoras' "Argument for Every
    Position"
Democritus' Atoms
Copernicus De-Centralization
Aquinas' Perfect Arguments
Descartes' Cartesian Coordinates
Locke's Materialism
Kant's Idealism
Hume's Empiricism
Newton's Calculus
James' Pragmatism
Einstein's Relativity
Whitehead's Process Philosophy
Wittgenstein's Atomic Facts
Popper's Objective Knowledge
Lewis' Many-Worlds Theory
Meillassoux's Radical
    Contingency

THE BOOK OF IDEAS

THE END (FOR NOW)

THE BOOK OF IDEAS

Nathan Coppedge

THE BOOK OF IDEAS

BIO

Nathan Coppedge is a philosopher, artist, inventor, and poet in some capacity. Jamal Martin calls him "[A] philosopher of this present age". He is the author of over 50 books, and one website lists him with the Top 100 Famous Quotations, right after Molière.

Readers of this book, please feel free to post a review on Amazon or Barnes & Noble. Also, look into other books by Nathan Coppedge.

www.ingramcontent.com/pod-product-compliance
Lightning Source LLC
Chambersburg PA
CBHW070230290526
45789CB00004B/1559